Food Chains and Habitats

by Ann Rossi

Food For Living Things

All living things need food. You need food. Animals need food. Plants need food too!

Frog

Gray squirrels

How Animals Get Food

Some animals eat plants. Rabbits eat plants. Some animals eat other animals. Lions eat other animals. Some animals eat plants and animals. Skunks eat fruit, seeds, insects, and mice.

How Plants Get Food

Plants use their parts to make food.
The leaves of green plants make food.
They use light from the Sun, air, and water.

Leaves

Stem

Roots

Sugar cane

Plant roots take in water. The stem takes water to the leaves. The green leaves take in sunlight and air. Now the green leaves have what they need to make food.

Food Chains

Plants make food, and food chains start. Plants give off oxygen when they make food. **Oxygen** is a gas in the air. Animals and plants need oxygen to live.

Animals find food in their habitats. They need to eat other living things. Some animals eat plants. Other animals eat those animals. The link between living things and the food they eat is a **food chain.**

Some jaguars
live in rain forests.

Food chains are in all habitats. A **rain forest** is a habitat. The Sun helps rain forest plants make food. Animals eat those plants. Other animals eat those animals. This makes a rain forest food chain.

A **marsh** is a wetland habitat. The Sun helps marsh plants make food too. Animals eat those plants. Other animals eat those animals. This makes a marsh food chain.

Some caimans live in marshes.

An Antarctic Food Chain

The Antarctic is a habitat. It is very cold. There are not as many living things there. But some plants and animals live in this habitat. Many live in the water.

The Antarctic has food chains. Food chains connect the living things of the Antarctic. They tell how living things find food there.

King penguins

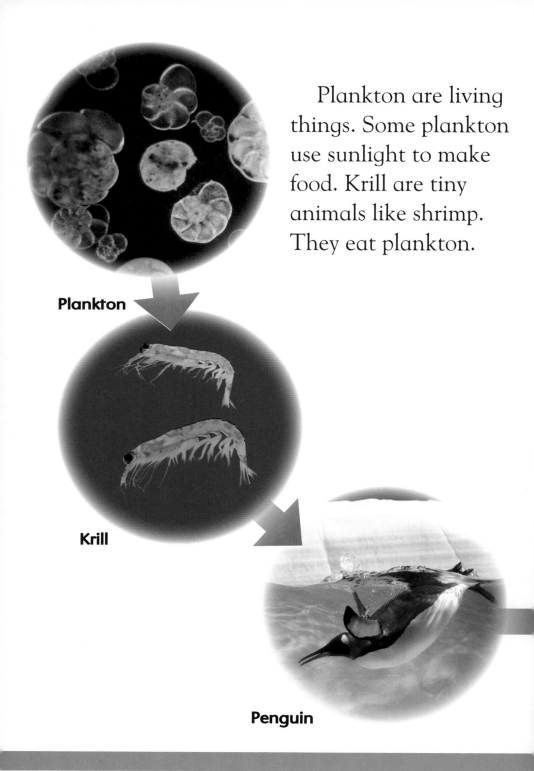

Plankton are living things. Some plankton use sunlight to make food. Krill are tiny animals like shrimp. They eat plankton.

Plankton

Krill

Penguin

Penguins eat krill. Penguins swim to get them. Orcas eat penguins they find in the water. This is an Antarctic food chain.

Orca

Living Things And Food Chains

Living things live in many habitats. Living things need to find food in their habitats.

Plants make their food. Some animals eat plants. Some animals eat other animals. Other animals eat plants and animals. All living things are connected in food chains.

Glossary

food chain   the connection between living things and their food

marsh   a wetland habitat

oxygen   a gas in the air that plants and animals need to live

rain forest   a habitat with tall trees and a lot of rain

What did you learn?

1. What three things do green leaves need to make food?

2. What does a penguin eat in the Antarctic?

3. **Writing** in Science Some animals eat other animals. On your own paper, write to tell which animals in this book eat other animals. Use words from the book as you write.

4. ⦿ **Draw Conclusions** Living things are connected in food chains. What happens if one part of a food chain changes?

Science

Genre	Comprehension Skill	Text Features	Science Content
Nonfiction	Draw Conclusions	• Call Outs • Captions • Labels • Glossary	Food Chains

Scott Foresman Science 1.5

ISBN 0-328-13746-4

9 780328 137466

90000